*In big ways
and small,
you can make
a difference
every day.*

Created By: _____

Date: _____

Never lose an opportunity of seeing anything beautiful, for beauty is God's handwriting.

Ralph Waldo Emerson

*Never lose an opportunity
of seeing anything beautiful, for beauty
is God's handwriting.*

Ralph Waldo Emerson

Created By: _____
Date: _____

Wisdom begins in wonder.
Socrates

Created By: _____
Date: _____

*The good things in life
   are meant to be shared.*

Created By: _____

Date: _____

*A friend may well be reckoned
the masterpiece of nature.*

Ralph Waldo Emerson

Created By: _____

Date: _____

Memories are the heart's way of keeping friends and family always close.

Created By: _____

Date: _____

Memories are the heart's way of keeping friends and family always close.

A gentle spirit can change the world.

Created By: _____
Date: _____

*There is only one happiness in this life,
to love and be loved.*
George Sand

Created By: _____
Date: _____

*Where we love is home—
home that our feet may leave,
but not our hearts.*

Oliver Wendell Holmes

Created By: _____
Date: _____

It's good to keep company
with those who see the
humorous side of life.

Created By: _____
Date: _____

*Animals are such agreeable friends—
    they ask no questions;
        they pass no criticisms.*

George Eliot

Created By: _____

Date: _____

The mere sense of living is joy enough.

Emily Dickinson

Created By: _____

Date: _____

Sometimes the best conversations are those when no words are spoken.

Created By: _____
Date: _____

If we all did the things we are capable of doing, we would literally astound ourselves.

Thomas Edison

Created By: _____

Date: _____

*Every great dream
begins with a dreamer.
Always remember,
you have within
you the strength,
the patience, and the
passion to reach for the
stars to change
the world.*

Harriet Tubman

Created By: _____

Date: _____

If I had to sum up friendship in one word, it would be comfort.

Terri Guillemets

Created By: _____

Date: _____

*The secret to humor
is surprise.*
Aristotle

Created By: _____
Date: _____

*Friendship is a treasure
of the heart.*

Created By: _____

Date: _____

We carry within us more strength, courage, and capability than we could ever imagine.

Created By: _____

Date: _____

Consider a day well-spent not by the amount you harvested, but by the number of seeds you planted.

Created By: _____

Date: _____

Good friends are the family we choose for ourselves.

*Good friends are the family
we choose for ourselves.*

Created By: _____
Date: _____

*Beauty may be said
to be God's trademark in creation.*

Henry Ward Beecher

Created By: _____
Date: _____

A multitude of small delights constitute happiness.

Charles Baudelaire

*A multitude of small delights
constitutes happiness.*

Charles Baudelaire

Created By: _____
Date: _____

And in the end...
The only thing
that really matters
is LOVE.

Created By: _____

Date: _____